LIVERPOOL
THE TROPHY YEARS

LIVERPOOL
THE TROPHY YEARS

PHIL THOMPSON & STEVE HALE

TEMPUS

First published 2003

Tempus Publishing Limited
The Mill, Brimscombe Port,
Stroud, Gloucestershire, GL5 2QG
www.tempus-publishing.com

British Library Cataloguing in Publication Data.
A catalogue record for this book is available from the British Library.

ISBN 0 7524 2951 5

Typesetting and origination by Tempus Publishing Limited.
Printed in Great Britain by Midway Colour Print, Wiltshire.

Roll of Honour

1893/94: Division Two Champions
1895/96: Division Two Champions
1900/01: League Champions
1904/05: Division Two Champions
1905/06: League Champions
1921/22: League Champions
1922/23: League Champions
1946/47: League Champions
1961/62: Division Two Champions
1963/64: League Champions
1964/65: FA Cup Winners
1965/66: League Champions
1972/73: UEFA Cup Winners
1972/73: League Champions
1973/74: FA Cup Winners
1975/76: League Champions
1975/76: UEFA Cup Winners
1976/77: League Champions
1976/77: European Cup Winners
1977/78: European Cup Winners
1977/78: European Super Cup Winners
1978/79: League Champions
1979/80: League Champions
1980/81: League Cup Winners
1980/81: European Cup Winners
1981/82: League (Milk) Cup Winners
1981/82: League Champions
1982/83: League Champions
1982/83: League (Milk) Cup Winners
1983/84: League (Milk) Cup Winners
1983/84: League Champions
1983/84: European Cup Winners
1985/86: League Champions
1985/86: FA Cup Winners
1987/88: League Champions
1988/89: FA Cup Winners
1989/90: League Championship Winners
1991/92: FA Cup Winners
1994/95: League (Coca-Cola) Cup Winners
2000/01: League (Worthington) Cup Winners
2000/01: FA Cup Winners
2000/01: UEFA Cup Winners
2001/02: European Super Cup Winners
2002/03: League (Worthington) Cup Winners

Above: Ray Kennedy holds the European Cup with jubilant team-mates Graeme Souness and Kenny Dalglish after Liverpool's victory over Bruges at Wembley 1978.

Below: Alan Hansen, Kenny Dalglish and Graeme Souness celebrate Liverpool's League (Milk) Cup victory over Everton in the replay at Maine Road, 1984.

Introduction

In their very first season in the Football League, Liverpool won the 1893/94 Second Division title. They have not stopped winning silverware since: forty-four major trophies in fact, making them the most successful club in the history of English football.

Liverpool really took off as a trophy-winning force when the legendary Bill Shankly arrived at the club in the late 1950s. After the halcyon days of Shankly, Paisley, Fagan and Dalglish, cups still kept finding their way into the Anfield trophy cabinet during the less successful periods when Souness and Evans were in control. In 2001 Gerard Houllier masterminded an incredible treble of League Cup, FA Cup and UEFA Cup successes. This book tells the story in words and pictures of each of Liverpool's trophy-winning triumphs in England and Europe, from the club's Second Division Championship success of 1894 through to their great victory over Manchester United in the 2003 League (Worthington) Cup final at the Millennium Stadium, Cardiff.

We would like to thank James Howarth, Kate Wiseman, Wendy Tse and all at Tempus Publishing.

Phil Thompson and Steve Hale
October 2003

1893/94
DIVISION TWO CHAMPIONS

Liverpool's first trophy-winning season was in 1893/94 when they won the Second Division Championship. Under the guidance of Belfast-born 'Honest John' McKenna they had a spectacular first season in the Football League and remained undefeated in 28 games. They won all of their fixtures at Anfield, scoring 26 goals and conceding just 6. Strictly speaking, McKenna was the Liverpool secretary, not the manager, but he performed many of the managerial duties at Anfield. Determined to see Liverpool installed in the Football League, McKenna reasoned that the best way of achieving his objective was to build a team that consisted mainly of Scottish-born talent. Liverpool became known as 'the team of Macs', with no fewer than thirteen 'Macs' in their squad. After winning the Second Division title, promotion was only gained to the First Division after Liverpool defeated Newton Heath (now known as Manchester United) 2-0 in a promotion deciding 'Test Match'.

Appearances: Bradshaw 14, Dewhurst 1, Dick 10, Givens 5, Gordon 21, Hannah 28, Henderson 21, Hughes 1, McBride 24, McCarthy 1, McCartney 16, McLean 28, McOwen 23, McQue 26, H. McQueen 27, M. McQueen 27, McVean 22, Stott 16, Worgon 1.

Goalscorers: Bradshaw 7, Dick 2, Givens 3, Hannah 1, Henderson 10, McBride 3, McCartney 1, McLean 5, McQue 2, H. McQueen 11, M. McQueen 1, Stott 14.

1895/96
DIVISION TWO CHAMPIONS

Liverpool were in the First Division for just one season before defeat against Bury in a 'Test Match' to determine if they would retain their status in the top flight sent them back down. They had finished the 1894/95 campaign in sixteenth place. The beginning of the 1895/96 season saw W.E. Barclay as the club's secretary/manager working alongside John McKenna as they attempted to bounce straight back into the First Division. McKenna predicted that Liverpool would return to the top flight within a year and his confidence was rewarded with another Second Division title. As was the case during their previous title-winning season, Liverpool were unbeatable at Anfield and during one game they notched up their record victory in the Football League. The 10-1 success over Rotherham Town in February 1896 created a club record that stands to this day. George Allan scored four as Liverpool ran riot. After competing in a series of 'Test Matches', Liverpool were promoted to the First Division for a second time.

Appearances: Allan 20, Battles 2, Becton 24, Bradshaw 26, Bull 1, Cleghorn 3, Curran 6, Dunlop 12, Geary 19, Goldie 22, Hannah 11, Holmes 17, Keech 6, McCartney 22, McLean 8, McQue 26, McVean 24, McQueen 22, Ross 25, Storer 11, Whitehead 2, Wilkie 21.

Goalscorers: Allan 25, Becton 17, Bradshaw 12, Geary 11, Hannah 3, McCartney 1, McQue 5, McVean 7, Ross 23, Storer 1, Wilkie 1.

Liverpool's first League title success came in the 1900/01 season. The team were now managed by Tom Watson, who has been described as one of football's first great managers. Watson had achieved notable success at his previous club, Sunderland, leading them to three title triumphs in the First Division. The lure of higher wages brought Watson to Anfield in 1896 in the role of secretary/manager.

Working alongside Watson at Liverpool was John McKenna, who was now the club chairman. After a few seasons consolidating themselves in the First Division, McKenna knew that Liverpool needed a boost on the playing side to push them into a challenging position for the title. Sticking to his favoured plan in the transfer market of signing the best Scottish talent that was available, McKenna heard that the outstanding defender Alex Raisbeck was available. With McKenna's prompting, Tom Watson travelled to Edinburgh to capture the tough-tackling defender. With Raisbeck in their line-up Liverpool's defence grew meaner, and after a great end-of-season run Liverpool captured the First Division Championship after a battle to the finish for the title with Sunderland. Liverpool needed a victory over West Brom in their final game at The Hawthorns and achieved it through a Walker goal. Liverpool Football Club had captured their first major trophy.

Appearances: Cox 32, Davies 1, Dunlop 32, Glover 11, Goldie 34, Howell 2, S. Hunter 8, T. Hunter 2, McGuigan 13, Parry 8, Perkins 34, Raisbeck 31, Raybould 31, J.T. Robertson 25, T. Robertson 34, Satterthwaite 22, Walker 29, Wilson 25.

Goalscorers: Cox 10, Goldie 2, S. Hunter 3, McGuigan 5, Raisbeck 1, Raybould 16, T.Robertson 9, Satterthwaite 5, Walker 7, Wilson 1.

1904/05
DIVISION TWO CHAMPIONS

After being relegated in 1904, Liverpool bounced straight back the following season as Second Division Champions. The Reds won 27 of their 34 games. The outstanding Raisbeck was again a key figure in the side as Liverpool ran riot as an attacking force, scoring 93 goals, with the Raisbeck-marshalled defence conceding just 25. Liverpool's most notable victory was an 8-1 drubbing of Burslem Port Vale. Manager Tom Watson had proved his credentials again, and the following season he would lead Liverpool to another League Championship success.

Appearances: Carlin 4, Chorlton 12, Cox 32, Doig 34, Dunlop 32, Fleming 29, Garside 1, Goddard 28, Hewitt 9, Hughes 4, Latham 1, Morris 7, Murray 12, Raisbeck 33, Raybould 32, Robinson 32, Parkinson 21, Parry 30, West 16, Wilson 5.

Goalscorers: Chorlton 3, Cox 10, Dunlop 2, Fleming 1, Goddard 7, Hewitt 1, Morris 1, Murray 1, Parkinson 20, Raisbeck 2, Raybould 20, Robinson 23, Own goals 1.

1905/06
LEAGUE CHAMPIONS

Liverpool became the first club to win the Second and First Division titles in successive seasons. Their 1905/06 campaign began badly with three straight defeats, most notably a 5-0 hammering at the hands of Aston Villa. After a 4-2 defeat against Everton at Goodison Park, few would have predicted that Tom Watson's Liverpool team would have a change in form, but as in 1900/01 the Reds turned their season round in dramatic style. A run of 10 wins in 11 games saw Liverpool rocket up the table. Crucial to Liverpool's change in fortune was the signing of goalkeeper Sam Hardy from Chesterfield for £500. Hardy proved a great success at Anfield and conceded just 26 goals in 30 games. Liverpool's top goalscorer in their title-winning season was Joe Hewitt with 23 goals. Liverpool's fine run of form saw them take the title by 4 points from nearest challengers Preston North End.

Appearances: Bradley 31, Carlin 14, Chorlton 6, Cox 28, Doig 8, Dunlop 31, Fleming 4, Garside 4, Goddard 38, Gorman 1, Griffiths 1, Hardy 30, Hewitt 37, Latham 5, Murray 3, Parkinson 9, Parry 36, Raybould 25, Raisbeck 36, Robinson 34, West 37.

Goalscorers: Carlin 6, Chorlton 1, Cox 8, Goddard 7, Hewitt 23, Parkinson 7, Parry 1, Raisbeck 1, Raybould 10, Robinson 11, West 3, Own goals 1.

Teddy Doig, who was Liverpool's goalkeeper when they won the Second Division title in 1905. Doig was nearing the end of his career when he joined the club in 1904, but he was crucial in their successful promotion-winning campaign. Doig retired in 1908.

Liverpool manager David Ashworth, who led Liverpool to the League Championship in 1922. Just a year later, Ashworth left Anfield to join Oldham Athletic, even though his team was on course to win a second successive title.

1921/22
LEAGUE CHAMPIONS

Liverpool's next championship success came in season 1921/22 under the managership of David 'Little Dave' Ashworth. Waterford-born Ashworth stood just 5'4" and became Liverpool boss in 1919. He produced one of the club's greatest ever teams, that included the legendary Elisha Scott in goal. Up front, Harold Chambers and Dick Forshaw scored the bulk of the goals at Liverpool. The Reds' championship victory was built on a strong defence, with Elisha Scott outstanding as Liverpool conceded just 36 goals in 42 games. It has to be remembered that during this period in English football history most teams leaked goals at an alarming rate compared to the modern game. Liverpool clinched the title with a 2–1 victory over defending champions Burnley in April 1922. Liverpool went on to take the championship by 6 points from runners-up Spurs.

Appearances: Bamber 8, Beadles 11, Bromilow 40, Chambers 32, Checkland 5, Cunningham 1, Forshaw 42, Gilhespy 2, Hopkin 42, Lacey 39, Lewis 19, Longworth 26, Lucas 27, McKinlay 29, McNab 29, Matthews 7, Mitchell 3, Parry 7, Scott 39, Shone 15, H. Wadsworth 1, W. Wadsworth 38.

Goalscorers: Beadles 6, Bromilow 2, Chambers 19, Forshaw 17, Gilhespy 1, Lacey 1, Lewis 1, Lucas 2, McKinlay 1, McNab 2, Matthews 4, Shone 6, Own goals 1.

The great Elisha Scott. Scott won two League Championship medals with Liverpool in 1922 and 1923 and is probably the only challenger to Ray Clemence as the greatest Liverpool goalkeeper of all time. He joined the club in 1912 and left in 1934, making 467 appearances for Liverpool. He also won 31 caps for Northern Ireland.

1922/23
LEAGUE CHAMPIONS

Liverpool retained their status as champions with another triumph in season 1922/23. David Ashworth had his team in top position in the league when he inexplicably decided to accept an offer from First Division rivals Oldham Athletic to take over the reins at the Lancashire club. Former Liverpool player Matt McQueen took over the manager's job mid-season and kept the club in control at the top until the campaign was over.

Liverpool's repeat title success once again owed a lot to the brilliant Elisha Scott, who conceded just 31 goals in 42 League appearances for the club that season. Chambers and Forshaw were again the goalscoring heroes up front. As was the case from the previous campaign, Liverpool won the title by a comfortable 6-point margin, this time from second-placed Sunderland.

Appearances: Bamber 4, Beadles 4, Bromilow 42, Chambers 39, Forshaw 42, Gilhespy 10, Hopkin 40, Johnson 37, Lacey 30, Longworth 41, Lucas 1, McKinlay 42, McNab 39, Pratt 7, Sambrooke 2, Scott 42, Shone 1, H. Wadsworth 3, W. Wadsworth 37.

Goalscorers: Bromilow 3, Chambers 22, Forshaw 19, Gilhespy 2, Hopkin 1, Johnson 14, Lacey 1, McKinlay 5, McNab 1, W. Wadsworth 2.

It had been a long wait since their 1923 triumph but the championship returned to Anfield in 1947. Liverpool's fifth title was achieved through solid, as opposed to spectacular, football. Jack Balmer and Albert Stubbins were the goalscoring stars in attack, with future legends Billy Liddell and Bob Paisley also key members of the team. Jack Balmer, in fact, became the first player to score three hat-tricks in consecutive League games during the 1946/47 season. Manager of Liverpool during this period in their history was George Kay. Kay had to guide his team to championship success against a backdrop of a season badly disrupted by a bitterly cold winter. The big freeze caused the postponement of many games and the season did not end until June. Because of the fixture pile-up, Liverpool found themselves playing their final four games away from home. Victory over Wolves at Molineux meant that only a Stoke victory at Sheffield United would deny the Anfield club. However, a 2-1 United victory over the Potteries club handed the championship to Liverpool, who won the trophy by a single point from Manchester United and Wolves, with Stoke back in fourth place.

Appearances: Ashcroft 2, Balmer 39, Bush 3, Carney 2, Done 17, Easdale 2, Estham 19, Fagan 18, Harley 17, Hughes 30, Jones 26, Kaye 1, Lambert 36, Liddell 35, McLeod 3, Minshull 6, Nieuwenhuys 15, Paisley 33, Polk 6, Priday 8, Ramsden 23, Sidlow 34, Spicer 10, Stubbins 36, Taylor 35, Watkinson 6.

Goalscorers: Balmer 24, Carney 1, Done 10, Fagan 7, Jones 2, Liddell 7, Nieuwenhuys 5, Priday 2, Stubbins 24, Taylor 1, Watkinson 1.

George Kay, the manager who led Liverpool to the First Division Championship in 1947. It was the club's first silverware since 1923 and would be Kay's only success in his stint as Liverpool boss.

Liverpool legend Billy Liddell. Liddell was a key member of the First Division Championship-winning team of 1947. Apart from making 537 appearances for Liverpool, scoring 229 goals, Liddell also won 28 caps for Scotland, and along with Stanley Matthews, was the only British player named in both Great Britain teams that took on the Rest of the World in the games of 1947 and 1955.

The transformation of Liverpool into one of the greatest clubs in the world began with the arrival at the club of the legendary Bill Shankly in 1959. Firstly, there was the small matter of getting out of the Second Division to take care of. Shankly's team achieved this in season 1961/62. They remained unbeaten at home for the entire season, and future England World Cup winner Roger Hunt created a club record of 41 league goals in a season. The arrival at the club of Ian St John and Ron Yeats gave Liverpool the edge on most of their Second Division rivals. Add to this the fact that Liverpool had future England internationals Hunt, Melia, Byrne and Callaghan in their ranks, plus the former England star Alan A'Court raiding on the wing, and it was obvious for all to see that the Anfield club were a First Division team in all but name. Liverpool's April 1962 victory over Southampton clinched promotion. The start of the club's insatiable appetite for accumulating silverware had begun.

Appearances: A'Court 42, Arrowsmith 1, Byrne 42, Callaghan 24, Furnell 13, Hunt 41, Leishman 41, Lewis 20, Melia 42, Milne 42, Molineux 3, Moran 16, Slater 29, St John 40, Wheeler 1, White 24, Yeats 41.

Goalscorers: A'Court 8, Byrne 1, Callaghan 1, Hunt 41, Leishman 1, Melia 12, Milne 2, Moran 1, St John 18, Own goals 4.

The start of Liverpool's rise to world fame. Bill Shankly's team wins the Second Division Championship in 1962. From left to right, back row: Bob Paisley, Gordon Milne, Jim Furnell, Tommy Leishman, Roger Hunt, Ian St John, Ian Callaghan. Front row: Ronnie Moran, Gerry Byrne, Alan A'Court, Ron Yeats, Liverpool chairman Tom Williams, president of the Football League Joe Richards, Bill Shankly, Jimmy Melia.

The jubilant Liverpool team parade around Anfield after their 1964 League Championship success.

1963/64
LEAGUE CHAMPIONS

Bill Shankly's first League Championship as manager came in the 1963/64 season. Liverpool fans had known about it for some time, but the rest of football now began to sit up and take notice of the Shankly Revolution taking place at Anfield. The superbly fit team began to take teams apart on their home patch. Arsenal, Aston Villa, Ipswich, Sheffield United and Wolves were all demolished by five or more goals. Once again, Roger Hunt hit a bagful of goals, as did Ian St John and Alf Arrowsmith, before injury blighted the unfortunate Arrowsmith's Liverpool career. With the outstanding wingers Peter Thompson and Ian Callaghan in the team it was small wonder that Liverpool's strike force ran riot at Anfield, scoring 60 goals in 21 games. Liverpool's Easter period of 1964 saw them emerge as potential champions after victories over Spurs (twice) and Leicester. Victory over Manchester United virtually secured the title, which they went on to win by 4 points from their Manchester rivals.

Appearances: Arrowsmith 20, Byrne 33, Callaghan 42, Ferns 18, Furnell 2, Hunt 41, Lawler 6, Lawrence 40, Melia 24, Milne 42, Moran 35, St John 40, Stevenson 38, P. Thompson 42, R. Thompson 2, Wallace 1, Yeats 36.

Goalscorers: Arrowsmith 15, Callaghan 8, Hunt 31, Melia 4, Milne 3, Moran 1, St John 21, Stevenson 1, Thompson 6, Yeats 1, Own goals 1.

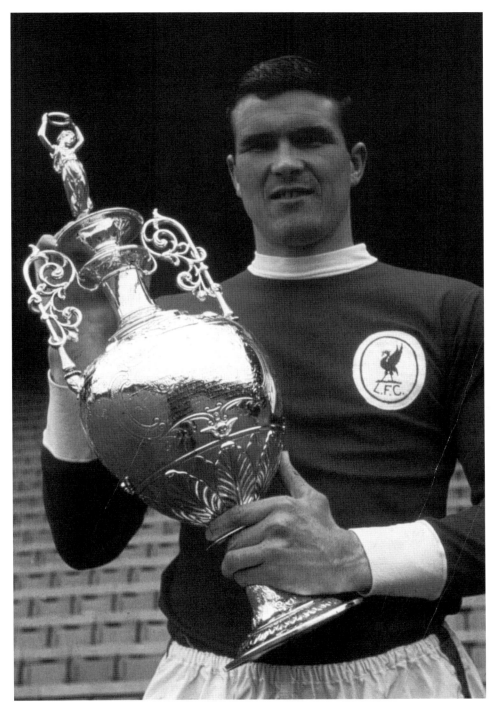

Liverpool captain Ron Yeats holds the First Division Championship trophy after his team's stunning title success in season 1963/64.

The Liverpool 1963/64 League Championship-winning line-up. From left to right, back row: Gordon Milne, Gerry Byrne, Tommy Lawrence, Ronnie Moran, Willie Stevenson, Bob Paisley (coach). Front row: Reuben Bennett (coach), Ian Callaghan, Roger Hunt, Ian St John, Tom Williams (chairman), Ron Yeats, Alf Arrowsmith, Peter Thompson, Bill Shankly (manager).

Peter Thompson, a great winger for Liverpool in Bill Shankly's trophy-winning teams of the 1960s. Thompson scored in Liverpool's 1965 FA Cup semi-final victory over Chelsea.

Liverpool won the FA Cup for the first time in their history in 1965. The Anfield faithful had waited seventy-three years to witness Liverpool achieving one of the English game's greatest honours. Some thought they would never win it, but that man Shankly delivered again. The final against Don Revie's Leeds United was not a classic, but Liverpool fans had had an abundance of attacking football to savour since Shankly arrived at the club. They just wanted their hands on the FA Cup – flair and dynamic attacking football could be put on hold for the time being. On a rainy, overcast day at Wembley in May 1965, Leeds made Liverpool scrap and fight every inch of the way for the trophy. The heroics of Gerry Byrne, who played for most of the game with a broken collarbone, have gone down into Anfield folklore. Goals from Hunt and St John gave the Reds a hard-fought 2–1 victory. It was estimated that over a million people lined the streets of Liverpool to welcome home their heroes. Liverpool have gone on to achieve a wealth of success in the domestic game and in European competition, but to older Liverpudlians this was the greatest trophy victory of all.

Round 3	West Bromwich Albion (a)	Won 2–1
Round 4	Stockport County (h)	Drew 1–1
Round 4 (replay)	Stockport County (a)	Won 2–0
Round 5	Bolton Wanderers (a)	Won 1–0
Round 6	Leicester City (a)	Drew 0–0
Round 6 (replay)	Leicester City (h)	Won 1–0
Semi-final	Chelsea (Villa Park)	Won 2–0
Final	Leeds United (Wembley)	Won 2–1 (aet)

Left: Liverpool legend Ian St John.
St John's goal won the FA Cup for
Liverpool in the 1965 final.

Below: Ian St John, a key figure in the
Liverpool trophy-winning teams of
the 1960s. Here, St John can be seen
in action against FC Cologne in
1965.

The Liverpool FA Cup-winning team of 1965. From left to right, back row: Ron Yeats, Gordon Milne (injured for the final), Willie Stevenson, Ian St John, Chris Lawler, Gerry Byrne. Front row: Tommy Lawrence, Peter Thompson, Geoff Strong, Tommy Smith, Roger Hunt, Ian Callaghan.

Bill Shankly's jubilant Liverpool team parade the FA Cup through the streets of Liverpool, 1965.

1965/66
LEAGUE CHAMPIONS

1966 was a fantastic time to be a football fan in Merseyside, with Liverpool winning the League Championship, Everton the FA Cup and England the World Cup. By now, the Shankly team had developed into the leading side in the country. After their 1966 title success, Liverpool chairman Sidney Reakes described his team as 'the kings of football'. Incredibly, Bill Shankly won Liverpool's seventh title using just fourteen players. Roger Hunt was in sensational goalscoring form, knocking in 30 goals in just 37 appearances. Liverpool's defence, magnificently led by Ron Yeats, with the rapidly maturing Tommy Smith playing alongside him, conceded only 34 goals. Liverpool took over at the top of the division in November and stayed there for the rest of the season. Once again the rest of football marvelled at the super-fit Liverpool team who seemed to play at full pace for the whole ninety minutes. Liverpool clinched the title with a victory over Tommy Docherty's Chelsea in April 1966. Leeds finished 6 points behind in the runners-up spot.

Appearances: Arrowsmith 5, Byrne 42, Callaghan 42, Graham 1, Hunt 37, Lawler 40, Lawrence 42, Milne 28, St John 41, Smith 42, Stevenson 41, Strong 22, Thompson 40, Yeats 42.

Goalscorers: Arrowsmith 1, Byrne 1, Callaghan 5, Hunt 30, Lawler 5, Milne 7, Smith 3, Stevenson 5, Strong 5, St John 10, Thompson 5, Yeats 2.

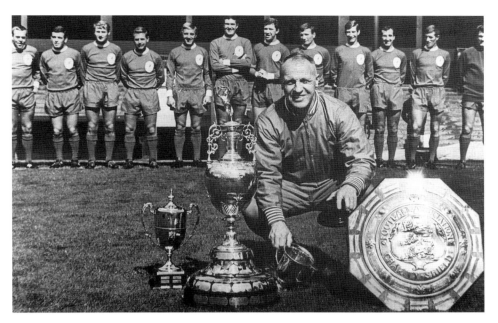

Bill Shankly with his First Division Championship trophy-winning team of 1966.

Peter Thompson, a key member of Shankly's title-winning team, 1966.

Opposite: The Liverpool First Division Championship-winning team of 1966. From left to right, back row: Gordon Milne, Gerry Byrne, Tommy Lawrence, Willie Stevenson, Chris Lawler. Front row: Ian Callaghan, Roger Hunt, Ron Yeats, Ian St John, Tommy Smith, Peter Thompson.

1972/73
UEFA CUP WINNERS

Liverpool's first success in European competition came in 1972/73 when they won the UEFA Cup. It would prove to be Bill Shankly's only capture of a European trophy. The team that he would leave behind, however, would go on to achieve success in Europe's greatest club competition, the European Cup. Liverpool had victories over such European opposition as Eintracht Frankfurt, Dynamo Berlin, AEK Athens and Dynamo Dresden before meeting the holders Spurs in the semi-final. Alec Lindsay gave Liverpool a narrow 1-0 victory in the home tie, but it took the away goals rule to put them through to the final. Spurs defeated the Reds 2-1, but Steve Heighway's crucial away goal counted double and Liverpool were through to their first European final. Liverpool had already secured the League title when they came up against Borussia Moenchengladbach over two legs in the UEFA Cup final of 1973. Shankly considered the Germans to be one of Europe's finest teams, so it came as no surprise that Liverpool were pushed all the way to win the trophy. A goal from Larry Lloyd and two from Keegan gave the Reds a 3-0 home victory, but the away leg proved a different matter. Borussia, inspired by German international stars Vogts, Netzer and Bonhof, tore Liverpool apart in the second leg and two goals from Heynekes saw Shankly's team desperately hanging on at the end to retain their one-goal lead.

Round 1, 1st leg	Eintracht Frankfurt (h)	Won 2-0
Round 1, 2nd leg	Eintracht Frankfurt (a)	Drew 0-0
Round 2, 1st leg	AEK Athens (h)	Won 3-0
Round 2, 2nd leg	AEK Athens (a)	Won 3-1
Round 3, 1st leg	Dynamo Berlin (a)	Drew 0-0
Round 3, 2nd leg	Dynamo Berlin (h)	Won 3-1
Round 4, 1st leg	Dynamo Dresden (h)	Won 2-0
Round 4, 2nd leg	Dynamo Dresden (a)	Won 1-0
Semi-final, 1st leg	Tottenham Hotspur (h)	Won 1-0
Semi-final, 2nd leg	Tottenham Hotspur (a)	Lost 2-1
Final, 1st leg	Borussia Moenchengladbach (h)	Won 3-0
Final, 2nd leg	Borussia Moenchengladbach (a)	Lost 0-2

Above: Liverpool's Chris Lawler, an outstanding servant for the club in the 1960s and '70s, seen here in action against Red Star Belgrade in 1973.

Right: Bill Shankly proudly holds the UEFA Cup after Liverpool won the trophy in 1973. This was to be Shankly's only European success.

The dynamic Steve Heighway, a key member of the Liverpool double trophy-winning team of 1973. Liverpool won the First Division title and the UEFA Cup.

1972/73
LEAGUE CHAMPIONS

Bill Shankly's last title success came in the 1972/73 season. By now, Shankly had rebuilt the Liverpool team with only Lawler, Smith and Callaghan remaining from his 1966 Championship-winning side. Outstanding talents such as Ray Clemence, Emlyn Hughes and Kevin Keegan were now leading Liverpool's pursuit of silverware, and Keegan in particular had emerged as the new darling of the Kop. Before the season began, Leeds and Manchester City were being talked of as potential champions, but it would be Liverpool and Arsenal who would fight it out for the title. Arsenal, in fact, briefly looked like favourites for the trophy after coming to Anfield in February 1973 and outplaying Liverpool for a 2-0 victory. But Shankly's 1973 team proved themselves as resilient as their outstanding 1960s counterparts and fought back to win the Championship with 3 points to spare over their London rivals.

Appearances: Boersma 19, Callaghan 42, Clemence 41, Cormack 30, Hall 21, Heighway 38, Hughes 41, Keegan 41, Lane 1, Lawler 42, Lindsay 37, Lloyd 42, Smith 33, Storton 4, Thompson 14, Toshack 22.

Goalscorers: Boersma 7, Callaghan 3, Cormack 8, Hall 2, Heighway 6, Hughes 7, Keegan 13, Lawler 3, Lindsay 4, Lloyd 2, Smith 2, Toshack 13, Own goals 2.

Bill Shankly leads his team on a victory parade at Anfield after Liverpool's 1973 League title success.

1973/74
FA CUP WINNERS

Bill Shankly's parting gift to his beloved Liverpool fans was the FA Cup in 1974. In one of the most one-sided FA Cup finals of all time, Liverpool were simply on a different planet to Newcastle United who appeared to freeze with fright on the day. Liverpool gave a virtuoso performance of power and precision passing as they swept Newcastle aside 3-0. Victories over Doncaster, Carlisle, Ipswich and Bristol City set up a semi-final tie against Leicester City. The first game resulted in a 0-0 stalemate, but in the replay at Villa Park, Kevin Keegan, giving his finest display in a Liverpool shirt, scored a wonder goal. With the sides drawing 1-1 in an evenly fought contest, Toshack put Keegan through the Leicester defence but he was still over twenty yards from goal. In a split second, Keegan, running at full speed, volleyed the ball with such force into the Leicester net that the astonished Shilton was barely given a chance to react to the shot. Liverpool went on to win the game 3-1 and book their FA Cup final place. In the final, Keegan was once again to the fore with two goals, the third coming from Steve Heighway. Bill Shankly knew that the formation of another great Liverpool team was now almost complete. When he handed over the managerial reins to Bob Paisley at the end of the 1973/74 season, the inspirational Scot was confident that the Anfield trophy-winning machine was in safe hands.

Round 3	Doncaster Rovers (h)	Drew 2-2
Round 3 (replay)	Doncaster Rovers (a)	Won 2-0
Round 4	Carlisle United (h)	Drew 0-0
Round 4 (replay)	Carlisle United (a)	Won 2-0
Round 5	Ipswich Town (h)	Won 2-0
Round 6	Bristol City (a)	Won 1-0
Semi-final	Leicester City (Old Trafford)	Drew 0-0
Semi-final (replay)	Leicester City (Villa Park)	Won 3-1
Final	Newcastle United (Wembley)	Won 3-0

Opposite above: Liverpool's Kevin Keegan is tackled by Newcastle's Terry McDermott during the 1974 FA Cup final. McDermott would later join Liverpool and enjoy many trophy-winning seasons at Anfield.

Opposite below: Ian Callaghan and Kevin Keegan hold the FA Cup after Liverpool demolished Newcastle 3-0 in the 1974 final.

Left: Liverpool's 1974 homecoming parade after their FA Cup success. Left to right: Bill Shankly, Steve Heighway, Emlyn Hughes, John Toshack.

Below: Two Liverpool legends, Bob Paisley and Bill Shankly, hold the FA Cup, 1974.

Season 1975/76 was the beginning of Bob Paisley's sensational trophy-winning run in his managerial reign at Liverpool. It has been well-documented that the modest Paisley did not really want the job when Shankly retired, but for the sake of the club he decided to 'give it a go'. Give it a go he did in incredible style, as one success followed another. Only two players from Shankly's first great team, Ian Callaghan and Tommy Smith, were still members of the side, but both would become European Cup-winners under Paisley. One of Paisley's many masterstrokes during his early period as Liverpool boss was to convert the former Arsenal striker Ray Kennedy into an international-class midfield player. Liverpool's ninth title success created a Football League record. It was only in their final game of the season that the League Championship was finally won. Liverpool needed to beat relegation threatened Wolves at Molineux to pip QPR, who had finished their League programme ten days earlier, by one point. Wolves took the lead, but Liverpool fought back through goals from Keegan, Toshack and Kennedy to bring the title to Anfield and condemn Wolves to relegation.

Appearances: Boersma 3, Callaghan 40, Case 27, Clemence 42, Cormack 17, Fairclough 14, Heighway 39, Hughes 41, Jones 13, Keegan 41, Kennedy 30, Kettle 1, Lindsay 6, McDermott 9, Neal 42, Smith 24, Thompson 41, Toshack 35.

Goalscorers: Callaghan 3, Case 6, Cormack 1, Fairclough 7, Hall 2, Heighway 4, Hughes 2, Keegan 12, Kennedy 6, McDermott 1, Neal 6, Toshack 16.

Jimmy Case, who scored vital goals from midfield after forcing his way into the Liverpool team in 1975.

Bob Paisley holds the First Division Championship trophy aloft after Liverpool's 1976 success. He would go on to win a further five League Championships for the club.

John Toshack, who along with Kevin Keegan, terrorized First Division defences during Liverpool's First Division title-winning campaign of 1975/76.

Kevin Keegan celebrates his goal against Manchester United at Anfield during the 1975/76 season. Liverpool beat United 3–1.

1975/76
UEFA CUP WINNERS

Liverpool's victory over Bruges in the final of the 1976 UEFA Cup gave Bob Paisley, in only his second season as manager, a double triumph. The newly crowned English champions equalled Leeds United's achievement in becoming only the second English club to win the UEFA Cup twice. In the first leg at Anfield, Bruges looked the more likely winners of the final when they raced into a two-goal advantage after just 12 minutes. Liverpool's trademark fighting spirit came to their rescue in the second-half when three strikes in a five-minute onslaught on the Bruges goal gave them a 3-2 victory. Ray Kennedy, Jimmy Case and Kevin Keegan saved Liverpool's blushes in the first game, and it was Keegan again in the second leg who equalised Bruges' early lead. Liverpool's superb defence held out for a 1-1 draw to give them their second European trophy. Manager Bob Paisley may have been unsure of his ability to make a success of replacing Shankly as manager, but after the tremendous double trophy-winning 1975/76 season, those doubts would never enter his head again.

Round 1, 1st leg	Hibernian (a)	Lost 0-1
Round 1, 2nd leg	Hibernian (h)	Won 3-1
Round 2, 1st leg	Real Sociedad (a)	Won 3-1
Round 2, 2nd leg	Real Sociedad (h)	Won 6-0
Round 3, 1st leg	Slask Wroclaw (a)	Won 2-1
Round 3, 2nd leg	Slask Wroclaw (h)	Won 3-0
Round 4, 1st leg	Dynamo Dresden (a)	Drew 0-0
Round 4, 2nd leg	Dynamo Dresden (h)	Won 2-1
Semi-final, 1st leg	Barcelona (a)	Won 1-0
Semi-final, 2nd leg	Barcelona (h)	Drew 1-1
Final, 1st leg	FC Bruges (h)	Won 3-2
Final, 2nd leg	FC Bruges (a)	Drew 1-1

Opposite: John Toshack seen here in action against Dynamo Dresden in the UEFA Cup in 1976.

Above: Kevin Keegan (partially hidden) blasts in a free kick to give Liverpool a 1-1 draw against Bruges in the second leg of the 1976 UEFA Cup final.

Right: John Toshack and Kevin Keegan celebrate Liverpool's 1976 UEFA Cup victory over Bruges.

Opposite: Emlyn Hughes holds the UEFA Cup aloft after Liverpool's success over Bruges in the 1976 UEFA Cup final, held over two legs. Liverpool won 4-3 on aggregate.

Ian Callaghan, who won a bagful of medals at Liverpool during the Shankly and Paisley years. During Liverpool's title-winning season of 1976/77, Callaghan made thirty-three appearances in the League.

1976/77
LEAGUE CHAMPIONS

1976/77 was probably the greatest season in Liverpool's history. At the end of it they would retain their League title, win the European Cup for the first time and narrowly miss out on a fabulous treble of success to a fluke goal by Manchester United in the 1977 FA Cup final. In the League, Liverpool tasted defeat in just 2 of their opening 16 games, and for the first time in a title-winning season, remained undefeated at Anfield. Liverpool retained the Championship by a narrow margin from Manchester City and Ipswich with a total of 57 points. They had not won it in the style they had hoped for, but the Reds were pushing for major silverware on three fronts and were happy to have their first objective, the League Championship, in the bag. The deciding factor for Liverpool was a run of games from the beginning of February to the end of the season which saw just two defeats, at Spurs and Bristol City. Liverpool's away form was in the main disappointing, but at Anfield they were unstoppable.

Appearances: Callaghan 33, Case 27, Clemence 42, Fairclough 20, Heighway 39, Hughes 42, Johnson 26, Jones 39, Keegan 38, Kennedy 41, Kettle 2, Lindsay 1, McDermott 26, Neal 42, Smith 16, Thompson 26, Toshack 22.

Goalscorers: Callaghan 1, Case 1, Fairclough 3, Heighway 8, Hughes 1, Johnson 5, Jones 3, Keegan 12, Kennedy 7, McDermott 1, Neal 7, Thompson 2, Toshack 10, Own goals 1.

1976/77
EUROPEAN CUP WINNERS

Liverpool's narrow 2-1 defeat to Manchester United in the 1977 FA Cup final left Bob Paisley and his staff with just a few days to lift Liverpool's spirits before the biggest game in the club's history, the 1977 European Cup final. Borussia Moenchengladbach were the opponents in Rome on 25 May. Just four days after their Wembley defeat, Paisley's team rose to the occasion, and after thirteen consecutive seasons of competing in Europe, they at last won the greatest prize of all. Against a Borussia team packed with international talent such as Vogts, Bonhof, Heynekes and the hugely-gifted Danish star Allon Simonsen, Liverpool were up against it. But with Liverpool's midfield of Case, Kennedy, Callaghan and McDermott taking control in the early stages, the Reds swarmed all over the Germans, and it was no surprise to see McDermott put them into the lead in the first half. Liverpool had looked irresistible and were confident of victory as they kicked off for the second half. A Simonsen goal for Borussia, however, put Liverpool on the back foot as the Germans began to dominate the second period. Ray Clemence had to be at his brilliant best to hold Borussia at bay as Liverpool regrouped. An unexpected headed goal from Tommy Smith, making his 600th Liverpool appearance, gave the Reds the lead again. A 3-1 victory was clinched when the superb Kevin Keegan, who had run Berti Vogts ragged all night, won a penalty which Phil Neal converted with the minimum of fuss. Liverpool were European champions for the first time after probably the greatest display in their history.

Round 1, 1st leg	Crusaders (h)	Won 2-0
Round 1, 2nd leg	Crusaders (a)	Won 5-0
Round 2, 1st leg	Trabzonspor (a)	Lost 0-1
Round 2, 2nd leg	Trabzonspor (h)	Won 3-0
Round 3, 1st leg	St Etienne (a)	Lost 0-1
Round 3, 2nd leg	St Etienne (h)	Won 3-1
Semi-final, 1st leg	FC Zurich (a)	Won 3-1
Semi-final, 2nd leg	FC Zurich (h)	Won 3-0
Final	Borussia Moenchengladbach (Rome)	Won 3-1

Opposite above: 16 March 1976: the moment David Fairclough became a Liverpool legend. Fairclough's 84th-minute winner against St Etienne of France put Liverpool into the European Cup semi-final, and after defeating FC Zurich in the semis, Liverpool were through to their first European Cup final.

Opposite below: Tommy Smith scores a sensational goal against Borussia Moenchengladbach to give Liverpool a 2-1 lead over the German champions in the 1977 European Cup final. A Phil Neal penalty gave the Reds a 3-1 victory. Liverpool's other goal was scored by McDermott.

Kevin Keegan gives German international defender Berti Vogts the runaround during Liverpool's victory over Borussia Moenchengladbach in the 1977 European Cup final.

Kevin Keegan, sporting a black eye, holds the European Cup the morning after Liverpool's magnificent 1977 success.

The red half of Liverpool goes crazy as their heroes parade the European Cup through the city streets, 1977.

Opposite: Liverpool's European Cup win of 1977 is celebrated by the people of Liverpool.

Right: Liverpool captain Emlyn Hughes displays the European Cup to the club's triumphant supporters at a civic reception, 1977.

1977/78
EUROPEAN CUP WINNERS

Liverpool retained the European Cup in 1977/78 with a 1-0 defeat of Belgian champions Bruges at Wembley. The Reds may have disappointed in their domestic campaign, but in Europe they were again the masters. With Kevin Keegan now departed to SV Hamburg for a record £500,000 fee, Kenny Dalglish was rapidly emerging as the new darling of the Kop. It was Dalglish who kept his cool to chip the ball over the advancing Bruges goalkeeper to win the European Cup for Liverpool in the 1978 final. On their way to the final Liverpool had an outstanding victory over Benfica, who were on a 46-game unbeaten run when Liverpool, through goals by Case and Hughes, beat then 2-1 at the Stadium of Light. Liverpool's 4-1 home victory at Anfield set up a semi-final against old adversaries Borussia Moenchengladbach. Liverpool, after a 2-1 away defeat, eased past the Germans with a comfortable 3-0 home success. Victory over Bruges in the final bestowed on Liverpool the distinction of becoming the first British club to retain the European Cup.

Round 1	Bye	
Round 2, 1st leg	Dynamo Dresden (h)	Won 5-1
Round 2, 2nd leg	Dynamo Dresden (a)	Lost 1-2
Round 3, 1st leg	Benfica (a)	Won 2-1
Round 3, 2nd leg	Benfica (h)	Won 4-1
Semi-final, 1st leg	Borussia Moenchengladbach (a)	Lost 1-2
Semi-final, 2nd leg	Borussia Moenchengladbach (h)	Won 3-0
Final	FC Bruges (Wembley)	Won 1-0

Kenny Dalglish chips the advancing Bruges goalkeeper to win the European Cup for Liverpool in the 1978 final. The game was played at Wembley and Liverpool became the first British Club to retain the trophy.

The Liverpool team celebrate their victory over Bruges in the European Cup final of 1978.

Opposite: Terry McDermott celebrates his hat-trick at Anfield against SV Hamburg in the European Super Cup, 1977. Liverpool won the trophy 7-1 on aggregate.

1977/78
EUROPEAN SUPER CUP WINNERS

European Cup-holders Liverpool took on European Cup Winners' Cup-holders SV Hamburg at the end of 1977 to decide which was the best team in Europe. By this time, former Anfield hero Kevin Keegan had joined Hamburg, with Kenny Dalglish taking his place in the Anfield team. In the first leg, played in Germany, Keller put Hamburg into the lead, but David Fairclough equalised for Liverpool to leave the tie evenly poised for the return leg at Anfield. Keegan was given a warm reception by the Liverpool fans as he stepped out onto the Anfield turf sporting a Hamburg shirt, but that was the end of any niceties as Liverpool thrashed the Germans 6-0. Terry McDermott scored a hat-trick and the game ended with the Kop chanting at Keegan, 'You should have stayed at Anfield'.

1st Leg
Team: Clemence, Neal, Jones (Smith), Thompson, R. Kennedy, Hughes, Dalglish, Case (Johnson), Heighway, Fairclough, Callaghan.
Result: Hamburg 1, Liverpool 1.
Goalscorer: Fairclough.

2nd Leg
Team: Clemence, Neal, Smith, Thompson, R. Kennedy, Hughes, Dalglish, Case, Heighway (Johnson), Fairclough, McDermott.
Result: Liverpool 6, Hamburg 0.
Goalscorers: McDermott 3, Thompson, Fairclough, Dalglish.

Liverpool's Ray Kennedy scores against Derby County at Anfield, 1978. Liverpool won the game 5-0.

1978/79
LEAGUE CHAMPIONS

Bob Paisley's fortieth season at Anfield was celebrated in style with an English record eleventh League title. Liverpool started the season with a six-game winning run, including the legendary 7-0 rout of Spurs – the heaviest defeat in the London club's seventy-year tenancy of the League. Liverpool hit top spot on just the second Saturday of the season and remained in pole position until the title was won. The key to Liverpool's 8-point winning margin from runners-up Nottingham Forest was the outstanding goalkeeping of Ray Clemence, who conceded just 16 goals in 42 games. Amazingly, Liverpool used just fifteen players during the 1978/79 campaign, two of whom (Lee and Fairclough) played only four games between them. Another record set by the team during this season (apart from the total of 68 points being a new First Division record) was a club record-breaking 30 League victories in a season. Liverpool remained unbeaten at Anfield and lost just 4 away games.

Appearances: Case 37, Clemence 42, Dalglish 42, Fairclough 4, Hansen 34, Heighway 28, Hughes 16, Johnson 30, A. Kennedy 37, R. Kennedy 42, Lee 2, McDermott 37, Neal 42, Souness 41, Thompson 39.

Goalscorers: Case 7, Dalglish 21, Fairclough 2, Hansen 1, Heighway 4, Johnson 16, R. Kennedy 10, A. Kennedy 3, McDermott 8, Neal 5, Souness 8.

1979/80
LEAGUE CHAMPIONS

It was once again fortress Anfield as Liverpool went through the entire 1979/80 season undefeated at home. Liverpool scored 46 goals with just 8 against in their 15 victories at Anfield. The outstanding Emlyn Hughes had now departed to Wolves, but the Liverpool defence was still as mean as ever. In the cup competitions Liverpool were found wanting, but in the League they still reigned supreme. David Johnson and Kenny Dalglish, ably assisted by Ray Kennedy and Terry McDermott from midfield, knocked in the bulk of the goals while Hansen, Thompson, Neal and Alan Kennedy gave little away at the back. With midfield tigers Jimmy Case and Graeme Souness dictating the play in the middle of the park, it was small wonder that most teams came away with nothing when they played Liverpool during this period. The Reds finished the season with a 2-point advantage over runners-up Manchester United.

Appearances: Case 37, Clemence 41, Cohen 4, Dalglish 42, Fairclough 14, Hansen 38, Heighway 9, Irwin 8, Johnson 37, A. Kennedy 37, R. Kennedy 40, Lee 7, McDermott 37, Neal 42, Ogrizovic 1, Souness 41, Thompson 42.

Goalscorers:: Case 3, Cohen 1, Dalglish 16, Fairclough 5, Hansen 4, Irwin 2, Johnson 21, A. Kennedy 1, R. Kennedy 9, McDermott 11, Neal 1, Souness 1, Own goals 6.

Ray Clemence, who was undoubtedly the finest Liverpool goalkeeper of the modern era. Clemence conceded just 4 goals at Anfield during the title-winning season of 1978/79. In 42 games he was beaten just 16 times.

Right: David Johnson scores at Anfield against West Brom at the start of the 1979/80 season. Liverpool beat the Midlands club 3-1 and remained unbeaten at home as they romped to yet another League Championship.

Below: Liverpool players celebrate with Kenny Dalglish after the second of his two goals in the 3-0 victory over Wolves at Anfield in 1979.

Liverpool won their first ever League Cup in the 1980/81 season, with a replay victory over West Ham in the final. It is hard to believe that the club had failed so many times in the lesser of the domestic competitions, but after they won it once they couldn't stop winning it. After a narrow semi-final success over two legs against Manchester City, Liverpool took the field against West Ham in the final, determined to win the trophy for the first time. Liverpool were led out by Ray Kennedy at Wembley, who skippered the Reds in place of the injured Phil Thompson. It was Kennedy's namesake Alan who opened the scoring, but Ray Stewart equalised to take the game to a replay at Villa Park. With future Liverpool legend Ian Rush playing only his second full game for the club, goals from Dalglish and Hansen gave Liverpool a 2-1 victory.

Round 2, 1st leg	Bradford City (a)	Lost 0-1
Round 2, 2nd leg	Bradford City (h)	Won 4-0
Round 3	Swindon Town (h)	Won 5-0
Round 4	Plymouth (h)	Won 4-1
Round 5	Birmingham City (h)	Won 3-1
Semi-final, 1st leg	Manchester City (a)	Won 1-0
Semi-final, 2nd leg	Manchester City (h)	Drew 1-1
Final	West Ham (Wembley)	Drew 1-1 (aet)
Final (replay)	West Ham (Villa Park)	Won 2-1

Opposite: Phil Thompson and Sammy Lee show the Kop the First Division Championship trophy after Liverpool's 1979/80 title success.

Right: The 'Bootroom' boys at Anfield. From left to right, back row: Ronnie Moran, Bob Paisley, Joe Fagan. Front row: Roy Evans, Tom Saunders, John Bennison.

Liverpool won the European Cup for the third time in the 1980/81 season. The Reds may have finished as also-rans in the fight for the First Division title, but in Europe they were in outstanding form. Ray Clemence played his last game for Liverpool in the final against Real Madrid before joining Spurs. It was estimated that over 12,000 Liverpool fans travelled to Paris for the final and there were no reports of any trouble. Liverpool were captained in the final by Phil Thompson, the Reds player who stood on the Kop as a boy. Liverpool had a relatively comfortable route to Paris, the only difficulty occurring when they came up against German opposition again in the semi-final in the shape of Bayern Munich. After a 0-0 stalemate at Anfield, Liverpool only reached the finals on the away goals rule after drawing 1-1 against the Germans in the second leg. The final against Real Madrid was far from a classic, but Liverpool and their fans just wanted their name on the trophy for a third time. The breakthrough came after a dour first-half when Alan Kennedy latched on to a Ray Kennedy throw-in, brushed past full-back Cortes and smashed the ball past the Madrid goalkeeper Agustin to win the European Cup for Liverpool. Bob Paisley had become the first manager to achieve a hat-trick of European Cup victories.

Round 1, 1st leg	Oulu Palloseura(a)	Drew 1-1
Round 1, 2nd leg	Oulu Palloseura (h)	Won 10-1
Round 2, 1st leg	Aberdeen (a)	Won 1-0
Round 2, 2nd leg	Aberdeen (a)	Won 4-0
Round 3, 1st leg	CSKA Sofia (h)	Won 5-1
Round 3, 2nd leg	CSKA Sofia (a)	Won 1-0
Semi-final, 1st leg	Bayern Munich (h)	Drew 0-0
Semi-final, 2nd leg	Bayern Munich (a)	Drew 1-1
Final	Real Madrid (Paris)	Won 1-0

Opposite: Sammy Lee established himself as a first-team regular during the 1980/81 season and was a key member of the Liverpool side that won the League Cup and European Cup double.

The Kop salute Bill Shankly during the early 1980s at Anfield.

Opposite above: Ray Kennedy, seen here in action against Alkmaar (1981/82 season). Kennedy was converted from a striker to a midfield player by Bob Paisley and became an outstanding performer for both Liverpool and England in his new role. He scored the vital away goal that took Liverpool through to the 1980/81 European Cup final.

Opposite below: Kenny Dalglish puts the Bayern Munich goal under pressure during the 1980/81 European Cup semi-final at Anfield. The game ended in a 0-0 draw but Liverpool drew the away leg 1-1 and went through to the final on the away goals rule.

Graeme Souness and manager Bob Paisley celebrate Liverpool's 1981 European Cup victory.

Opposite above: Alan Kennedy scores the goal that defeated Real Madrid in the 1981 European Cup final. Liverpool won the game 1-0.

Opposite below: Liverpool's hero Alan Kennedy with the European Cup after his goal gave them victory over Real Madrid, 1981.

The most successful manager in English football history, Bob Paisley, with a table full of trophies.

Opposite above: Alan Hansen celebrates Liverpool's victory over Real Madrid in the 1981 European Cup final.

Opposite below: Liverpool match-winner Alan Kennedy with a smiling manager Bob Paisley after the European Cup final in Paris, 1981. Kennedy's goal gave Liverpool a 1-0 victory over Real Madrid.

1981/82
LEAGUE (MILK) CUP WINNERS

Liverpool's second League Cup success came after a hard-fought final against Spurs. The 1981/82 League Cup final looked like seeing the London club retain their record of never losing in a Wembley final. Steve Archibald opened the scoring in the 11th minute, and Spurs held the lead until the final few minutes when Ronnie Whelan shot past his former team-mate Ray Clemence to level the score. The Tottenham players visibly wilted and it was no surprise to see Liverpool take control in extra time. Goals from Whelan and Rush saw the Reds retain the trophy, becoming only the second team to achieve this feat in the process.

Round 2, 1st leg	Exeter City (h)	Won 5-0
Round 2, 2nd leg	Exeter City (a)	Won 6-0
Round 3	Middlesborough (h)	Won 4-1
Round 4	Arsenal (a)	Drew 0-0
Round 4 (replay)	Arsenal (h)	Won 3-0
Round 5	Barnsley (h)	Drew 0-0
Round 5 (replay)	Barnsley (a)	Won 3-1
Semi-final, 1st leg	Ipswich Town (a)	Won 2-0
Semi-final, 2nd leg	Ipswich Town (h)	Drew 2-2
Final	Tottenham H (Wembley)	Won 3-1 (aet)

With Bruce Grobbelaar taking Ray Clemence's place in goal and Mark Lawrenson installed in defence, Bob Paisley's all-conquering 1970s team was gradually being rebuilt, but they were still as consistent as ever. Ian Rush's partnership with Dalglish up front looked to be a combination made in heaven as Liverpool gradually made up lost ground in the 1981/82 title chase after a poor start to the season. Liverpool, in fact, tasted success in just 6 of their first 17 games and started the New Year in twelfth position in the table. However, a fantastic second half to the season saw them rocket up the League, and they remained undefeated in their final 16 games. Liverpool won their thirteenth League Championship by 4 points from Ipswich, with Manchester United 9 points behind in third position. Bob Paisley declared that he was particularly proud of this title success because of the way his team had fought back after such a poor start to the season.

Appearances: Dalglish 42, Grobbelaar 42, Hansen 35, Johnson 15, Johnston 18, A. Kennedy 34, R. Kennedy 15, Lawrenson 39, Lee 35, McDermott 29, Neal 42, Rush 32, Sheedy 2, Souness 35, P. Thompson 34, Whelan 32.

Goalscorers: Dalglish 13, Johnson 2, Johnston 6, A. Kennedy 3, R. Kennedy 2, Lawrenson 2, Lee 3, McDermott 14, Neal 2, Rush 17, Souness 5, Whelan 10, Own goals 1.

Kenny Dalglish scores in Liverpool's 3-1 victory over Spurs that clinched the 1981/82 League Championship.

Phil Neal is carried from the pitch by ecstatic Liverpool fans after his team had just beaten Spurs to win another League Championship, 1982.

Opposite: Bruce Grobbelaar, the enigmatic goalkeeper who took over from Ray Clemence in the Liverpool goal at the start of the 1981/82 season.

Liverpool's Phil Thompson proudly holds the 1981/82 League Championship trophy aloft.

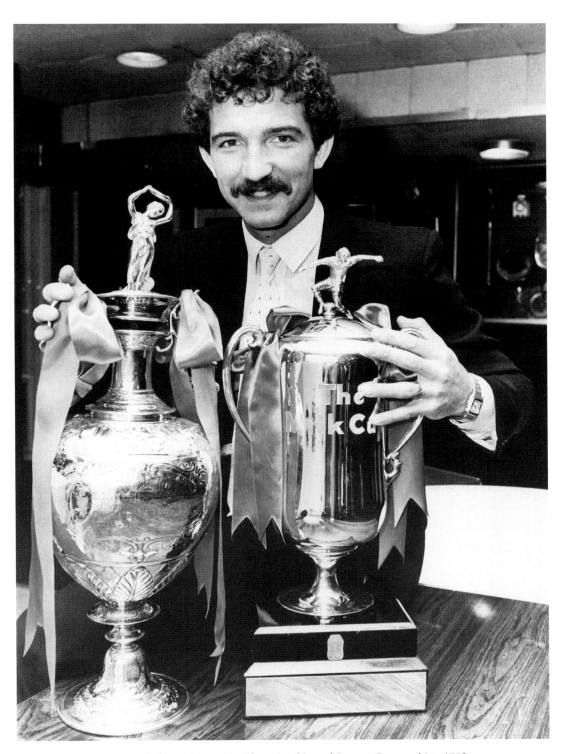

Graeme Souness with the First Division Championship and League Cup trophies, 1982.

1982/83
LEAGUE CHAMPIONS

Bob Paisley's final season as manager saw the club win their fourteenth League Championship. The 1982/83 title victory was Paisley's sixth as manager. When you take into account the seven other major trophies that he brought to Anfield during his reign, Paisley's total is unlikely to ever be bettered at the club. The Rush/Dalglish partnership was by now in full flow, and between them they scored 42 League goals as Liverpool swept to an easy Championship success. Newly promoted Watford were the surprise package that 1982/83 season, but even they finished 11 points behind the Reds. Unbelievably, Liverpool actually lost 5 of their final 7 games as they coasted through their end-of-season fixtures with the League Championship in the bag.

Appearances: Dalglish 42, Fairclough 8, Grobbelaar 42, Hansen 34, Hodgson 23, Johnston 33, A. Kennedy 42, Lawrenson 40, Lee 40, McDermott 2, Neal 42, Nicol 4, Rush 34, Souness 41, P. Thompson 24, Whelan 28.

Goalscorers: Dalglish 18, Fairclough 3, Hodgson 4, Johnston 7, Kennedy 3, Lee 3, Lawrenson 5, Neal 8, Rush 24, Souness 9, Whelan 2.

Opposite: Bob Paisley won his sixth League Championship as Liverpool manager in the 1982/83 season. Back in the sanctuary of the Liverpool bootroom he can hardly contain his happiness.

Bob Paisley receiving the First Division Championship trophy with his team, 1983.

Opposite: The outstanding Alan Hansen celebrates Liverpool's 1982/83 League Championship triumph.

1982/83
LEAGUE (MILK) CUP WINNERS

Liverpool completed a hat-trick of League Cup victories with a 2-1 defeat of Manchester United in the 1983 final. Goals from Alan Kennedy and Ronnie Whelan won the day for Liverpool. United actually took the lead when Norman Whiteside became the youngest scorer in a League Cup final. However, injuries to Moran and McQueen decimated the United defence and Liverpool's continual probing paid off in the 75th minute when Kennedy equalised. Whelan's extra-time winner gave Liverpool the cup, and it was Bob Paisley who climbed the famous Wembley steps to hold the trophy aloft on his last Wembley visit as a team manager. He became the first manager in Wembley history to be accorded this richly deserved accolade.

Round 2, 1st leg	Ipswich Town (a)	Won 2-1
Round 2, 2nd leg	Ipswich Town (h)	Won 2-0
Round 3	Rotherham United (h)	Won 1-0
Round 4	Norwich City (h)	Won 2-0
Round 5	West Ham United (h)	Won 2-1
Semi-final, 1st leg	Burnley (h)	Won 3-0
Semi-final, 2nd leg	Burnley (a)	Lost 0-1
Final	Manchester United (Wembley)	Won 2-1 (aet)

Ronnie Whelan's extra-time winner leaves Manchester United goalkeeper Gary Bailey well beaten as Liverpool win the 1983 League Cup final 2-1.

Bob Paisley became the first manager in Wembley history to climb the famous steps to collect a trophy when he was accorded this richly deserved accolade after Liverpool won the League Cup in 1983.

1983/84
LEAGUE (MILK) CUP WINNERS

Bootroom boy Joe Fagan took over from Bob Paisley at the end of the 1982/83 season, and there was still no end to the stream of trophies finding their way to the Anfield trophy cabinet. The first of Fagan's sensational treble of cups was the 1984 League Cup. In the first all-Merseyside Wembley final in history, Liverpool drew with neighbours Everton 0-0, but defeated the Blues 1-0 in the Maine Road replay. The nation was astonished to witness the camaraderie between the two sets of supporters as they took over the capital for the day without a hint of the hatred and violence that had marred English football for decades. On the field of play it was no-holds-barred stuff as the two teams ground out a goal-less draw. It took a special Graeme Souness goal to win the day for the Reds in the replay. The 1-0 victory sent the red half of the city into ecstasy and the blue half into mourning.

Round 2, 1st leg	Brentford (a)	Won 4-1
Round 2, 2nd leg	Brentford (h)	Won 4-0
Round 3	Fulham (a)	Drew 1-1
Round 3 (replay)	Fulham (h)	Drew 1-1 (aet)
Round 3 (2nd replay)	Fulham (a)	Won 1-0 (aet)
Round 4	Birmingham City (a)	Drew 1-1
Round 4 (replay)	Birmingham City (h)	Won 3-0
Round 5	Sheffield Wednesday (a)	Drew 2-2
Round 5 (replay)	Sheffield Wednesday (h)	Won 3-0
Semi-final, 1st leg	Walsall (h)	Drew 2-2
Semi-final, 2nd leg	Walsall (a)	Won 2-0
Final	Everton (Wembley)	Drew 0-0 (aet)
Final (replay)	Everton (Maine Road)	Won 1-0

Opposite: Ronnie Whelan is carried from the pitch by jubilant Liverpool fans after their 1984 Milk Cup final replay victory over Everton.

Above: Liverpool captain Graeme Souness celebrates his goal against rivals Everton in the League Cup final replay at Maine Road, 1984. Liverpool won the game 1-0.

Left: Graeme Souness with the League (Milk) Cup, 1984.

Opposite: Joe Fagan took over as Liverpool manager at the start of the 1983/84 season. He won an incredible three trophies in his first season in charge.

Liverpool emulated the great Huddersfield and Arsenal teams of the pre-war era by achieving a hat-trick of Championships in the 1983/84 season. In his first season in charge, Joe Fagan now had two major trophies to his name with an even bigger prize still to come. Ian Rush in particular was in sensational form in the League with 32 goals to his name. Liverpool's fifteenth Championship was, however, a far from easy success with the main challengers being surprise package Southampton. Only 3 points separated the two clubs at the end of the campaign, with Nottingham Forest 6 points behind the Reds in third place. There had been some who had doubted Joe Fagan's ability to step into the manager's job after the sensational Bob Paisley had retired. It was quite clear that the well-oiled trophy winning machine at Anfield was still functioning at maximum speed.

Appearances: Dalglish 33, Grobbelaar 42, Hansen 42, Hodgson 5, Johnston 29, A. Kennedy 42, Lawrenson 42, Lee 42, Neal 42, Nicol 23, Robinson 24, Rush 41, Souness 37, Wark 9, Whelan 23.

Goalscorers: Dalglish 7, Hansen 1, Johnston 2, A. Kennedy 2, Lee 2, Neal 1, Nicol 6, Robinson 6, Rush 32, Souness 7, Wark 2, Whelan 3, Own goals 2.

Above: Alan Hansen, who was an ever-present in Liverpool's 1983/84 title-winning team.

Opposite above: Ian Rush scores against Aston Villa at the start of the 1983/84 season.

Opposite below: The pressures of a Liverpool *v.* Everton derby get to Joe Fagan during the 1983/84 season.

Liverpool's victory in the 1984 European Cup final over AS Roma was the final leg of Joe Fagan's sensational treble of trophies in his first season as manager. Liverpool won the trophy for the fourth time after extra time and then penalties decided the issue. To have come out victorious against a Roma team playing on their home ground at the Olympic Stadium in Rome was one of Liverpool's greatest achievements in Europe. On their way to the final Liverpool produced some amazing displays, most notably the stunning 4–1 victory over Benfica in the away leg of the tie. Liverpool were in fact outstanding in all of the away ties on their way to the final, beating BK Odense, Athletic Bilbao and Dinamo Bucharest as well as Benfica. In the final itself, Phil Neal gave Liverpool an early lead against Roma, but Pruzzo equalised just before half-time. With the remainder of the ninety minutes and extra time failing to produce a winner, it was Liverpool who kept their nerve better in the penalty shoot-out with Alan Kennedy netting the vital kick that took the European Cup back to Anfield.

Round 1, 1st leg	BK Odense (a)	Won 1–0
Round 1, 2nd leg	BK Odense (h)	Won 5–0
Round 2, 1st leg	Athletic Bilbao (h)	Drew 0–0
Round 2, 2nd leg	Athletic Bilbao (a)	Won 1–0
Round 3, 1st leg	Benfica (h)	Won 1–0
Round 3, 2nd leg	Benfica (a)	Won 4–1
Semi-final, 1st leg	Dinamo Bucharest (h)	Won 1–0
Semi-final, 2nd leg	Dinamo Bucharest (a)	Won 2–1
Final	AS Roma (Rome)	Won 4–2 on penalties after 1–1 draw

Opposite above: The Liverpool team parade the League Championship trophy around Anfield, 1984.

Opposite below: The Liverpool team celebrate their League Championship success of the 1983/84 season. From left to right, back row: Bruce Grobbelaar, Ronnie Whelan, Ian Rush, Alan Hansen, Kenny Dalglish, Mark Lawrenson, Craig Johnston, Phil Thompson. Front row: Sammy Lee, Graeme Souness, Phil Neal.

Kenny Dalglish scores against BK Odense of Denmark in the European Cup first-round game at Anfield, 1983.

Liverpool's Michael Robinson lobs a shot goalward over crouching team-mate Ian Rush against Athletic Bilbao in the European Cup, 1983/84 season. Liverpool won the tie 1-0 on aggregate.

Phil Neal scores against AS Roma in the European Cup final 1984. Liverpool won the trophy 4-2 on penalties after extra-time failed to find a winner.

Liverpool parade their three trophies through the streets of Liverpool, 1984.

The victorious Liverpool side after their victory over AS Roma in the European Cup final, 1984. From left to right, back row: Mike Hooper, Bruce Grobbelaar, Kenny Dalglish, Steve Nicol, Alan Hansen, Mick Robinson, Gary Gillespie, Mark Lawrenson, Ronnie Moran (coach), Ian Rush, Tom Saunders (youth development officer). Front row: Ronnie Whelan, Phil Neal, Sammy Lee, Graeme Souness, Craig Johnston, Alan Kennedy, David Hodgson.

Opposite: One of his proudest moments in football: Ian Rush with the European Cup, 1984.

Left: Phil Neal proudly holds up the European Cup, 1984.

Below: The Liverpool team parade their treble trophy haul through the streets of Liverpool, 1984.

The victory parade reaches Liverpool's Lime Street, 1984.

1985/86
LEAGUE CHAMPIONS

With Kenny Dalglish now at the helm, he emulated his predecessor Joe Fagan by winning the League Championship in his first season in charge. Liverpool's 1985/86 title victory was a hard-fought affair with Everton pushing the Reds all the way in both the League and FA Cup. It was the Goodison Park club who looked to be in the driving seat all season, but a sensational Liverpool run of 11 wins and a draw in their final 12 games saw the Reds pip Everton by 2 points, with West Ham 4 points behind Liverpool in third spot. It was the player-manager Kenny Dalglish himself who decided the issue when he scored the vital goal that meant that his team could not be caught by Everton in the chase for the title. It was Liverpool's sixteenth League Championship success.

Appearances: Beglin 34, Dalglish 21, Gillespie 24, Grobbelaar 42, Hansen 41, Johnston 42, A. Kennedy 8, Lawrenson 38, Lee 15, McMahon 23, MacDonald 17, Molby 39, Neal 13, Nicol 34, Rush 40, Walsh 20, Wark 9, Whelan 39.

Goalscorers: Beglin 1, Dalglish 3, Gillespie 3, Johnston 7, Lawrenson 3, McMahon 6, MacDonald 1, Molby 14, Neal 1, Nicol 1, Rush 22, Walsh 11, Wark 3, Whelan 10.

When Kenny Dalglish accepted Liverpool's offer to become club manager, few would have predicted that he would lead his team to the 'double', but Liverpool's 1986 FA Cup victory over Everton saw them become only the third club to complete this feat in the twentieth century. The Merseyside giants were undoubtedly the two best teams in the country, and few could separate them when choosing a winner for the final. Everton had the superb Gary Lineker leading their attack, but Liverpool had the equally gifted Ian Rush ready to strike for them. Once again, London was invaded by Liverpool and Everton's red and blue armies, with Evertonians praying that they would not witness Liverpool clinching the 'double' at the expense of their heroes. As it turned out, the game was a thriller with first Everton and then Liverpool seizing the initiative. Lineker's opening goal was equalised by Rush in the early stages of the second half. Craig Johnston then shot Liverpool into the lead as the Anfield team began to dominate. The outstanding Jan Molby orchestrated wave after wave of Liverpool's attacking moves, and it was no surprise to see Ian Rush end any hopes of an Everton comeback with a third goal for the Reds in the final stages of the game. Manager Kenny Dalglish was already a living legend at Anfield; now he was immortal.

Round 3	Norwich City (h)	Won 5-0
Round 4	Chelsea (a)	Won 2-1
Round 5	York City (a)	Drew 1-1
Round 5 (replay)	York City (h)	Won 3-1 (aet)
Round 6	Watford (h)	Drew 0-0
Round 6 (replay)	Watford (a)	Won 2-1 (aet)
Semi-final	Southampton (White Hart Lane)	Won 2-0
Final	Everton (Wembley)	Won 3-1

Opposite: Steve Nicol, an outstanding player for Liverpool during the 1980s.

Right: Liverpool legend Kenny Dalglish took over as team manager at the start of the 1985/86 season. Here, Dalglish can be seen in the Liverpool dugout with Ronnie Moran and Roy Evans.

Below: Kenny Dalglish scores the goal at Chelsea that clinched the 1985/86 League title.

Left: Two great Merseyside footballers who went on to become outstanding managers, Kenny Dalglish and Everton's Howard Kendall. Dalglish had just been presented with the 'Manager of the Year' award, 1986.

Below: Ian Rush scores the first of his two goals that broke Everton's hearts at Wembley in the 1986 FA Cup final.

Ian Rush fires in the second goal that secured a 3–1 victory for Liverpool against Everton in the 1986 FA Cup final.

Right: Liverpool player–manager Kenny Dalglish holds the FA Cup aloft at Wembley, 1986. If Dalglish was already a living legend, he was now immortal. Liverpool had won the League and FA Cup 'double' for the first time in their history.

Below: The Liverpool FA Cup winning squad, 1986. From left to right, back row: Bruce Grobbelaar, Kenny Dalglish, Gary Gillespie, Jan Molby, Mike Hooper, Mark Lawrenson, Ian Rush, Kevin MacDonald, Ronnie Whelan, John Wark. Middle row: Paul Walsh, Sammy Lee. Front row: Steve McMahon, Craig Johnston, Jim Beglin, Alan Hansen, Steve Nicol.

Above: Kenny Dalglish holds the FA Cup and League Championship trophy during Liverpool's triumphant homecoming tour of Liverpool, 1986.

Left: Kenny Dalglish kisses the League Championship trophy during Liverpool's victory parade, 1986.

Opposite: Kenny Dalglish holds the League Championship trophy aloft at Anfield, 1986.

Liverpool and Everton share the Charity Shield at Wembley after a 1-1 draw, 1986.

1987/88
LEAGUE CHAMPIONS

With John Aldridge netting 26 League goals, Liverpool hardly missed Ian Rush, who was now plying his trade in Italy. The Reds stormed to the 1987/88 League Championship playing a brand of attacking football that had the purists drooling with pleasure. John Barnes and Peter Beardsley were at the height of their powers as Liverpool went on a 29-game unbeaten run from the start of the season. It was not until the Reds met local rivals Everton on 16 March that they tasted their first defeat of the season, losing 1-0 to a Wayne Clark goal. Liverpool had equalled the 29-game unbeaten run of Don Revie's 1973/74 Leeds team, but the Goodison Park defeat stopped them establishing a new record. All of this was immaterial to Dalglish's team as they won a seventeenth League Championship by 9 points from Manchester United, with Nottingham Forest 17 points behind Liverpool in third place. After a fabulous display in their 5-0 drubbing of Nottingham Forest, soccer legend Sir Tom Finney described the 1987/88 side as probably the best team of all time. Few who witnessed them in action that night against Forest would disagree with Sir Tom's sentiments.

Appearances: Ablett 17, Aldridge 36, Barnes 38, Beardsley 38, Dalglish 2, Gillespie 35, Grobbelaar 38, Hansen 39, Hooper 2, Houghton 28, Johnston 30, Lawrenson 14, MacDonald 1, McMahon 40, Molby 7, Nicol 40, Spackman 27, Venison 18, Walsh 8, Wark 1, Watson 2, Whelan 28.

Goalscorers: Aldridge 26, Barnes 15, Beardsley 15, McMahon 9, Nicol 6, Houghton 5, Johnston 5, Gillespie 4, Hansen 1, Whelan 1.

John Aldridge celebrates after scoring in Liverpool's 5-0 demolition of Nottingham Forest in the Reds' Championship-winning season of 1987/88.

The Liverpool squad of the 1987/88 season. One writer described them as 'better than the Brazilians'. Liverpool lost only two League games during the entire season and set a club record with 90 points. The team were also unbeaten in a 19-game run, equalling Leeds' achievement set in the 1973/74 season. From left to right, back row: Kenny Dalglish, Roy Evans (coach), Kevin MacDonald, Barry Venison, Jan Molby, Ronnie Whelan, Mike Hooper, John Barnes, Craig Johnston, Nigel Spackman, Gary Gillespie, Bruce Grobbelaar, Ronnie Moran (coach), Sir John Smith (Chairman). Front row: Jim Beglin, John Aldridge, Steve McMahon, Peter Beardsley, Alan Hansen, Steve Nicol, Ray Hougthon, Gary Ablett.

1988/89
FA CUP WINNERS

In a season dominated by the appalling Hillsborough tragedy, Liverpool won the 1989 FA Cup final against Everton, but few really cared. After Hillsborough there were calls for the competition to be scrapped for that season, but in honour of their fans, Liverpool continued in the FA Cup. After victory over Nottingham Forest in the replayed semi-final, Wembley once again hosted an all-Merseyside final. With Ian Rush now back at Anfield after his brief stay at Juventus, Liverpool were favourites to take the trophy. It was in fact Rush who won the day for Liverpool with two extra-time goals. Liverpool had led from as early as the fourth minute when John Aldridge gave the Reds a dream start. Everton battled for the equaliser and Stuart McCall struck with a minute to go to take the game into extra time. McCall scored again for Everton, but Rush's goals gave Liverpool their fourth success in the competition. The FA Cup was back at Anfield after an emotional day at Wembley.

Round 3	Carlisle United (a)	Won 3-0
Round 4	Millwall (a)	Won 2-0
Round 5	Hull City (a)	Won 3-2
Round 6	Brentford (h)	Won 4-0
Semi-final	Nottingham Forest (Old Trafford)	Won 3-1
Final	Everton (Wembley)	Won 3-2 (aet)

1989/90
LEAGUE CHAMPIONSHIP WINNERS

Kenny Dalglish's last trophy as Liverpool manager was the 1989/90 League Championship. Liverpool won the title for the eighteenth time in a season that saw them establish their record First Division victory with a 9-0 thrashing of Crystal Palace. Once again John Barnes was in sparkling form, finishing top scorer with 22 League goals. Liverpool's closest rivals Aston Villa trailed the Reds by 9 points at the end of the season, as Dalglish's team romped to a comfortable title success. Dalglish, by now 39 years of age, even found time to make a farewell appearance for Liverpool when he played against Derby County at Anfield on the night they were presented with the trophy. Although he only made 8 appearances for Liverpool that season, Ronny Rosenthal scored 7 League goals to help his team's end-of-season push for the title.

Appearances: Ablett 15, Aldridge 2, Barnes 34, Beardsley 29, Burrows 26, Dalglish 1, Gillespie 13, Grobbelaar 38, Hansen 31, Houghton 19, Hysen 35, McMahon 38, Marsh 2, Molby 17, Nicol 23, Rosenthal 8, Rush 36, Staunton 20, Tanner 4, Venison 25, Whelan 34.

Goalscorers: Aldridge 1, Barnes 22, Beardsley 10, Gillespie 4, Houghton 1, Hysen 1, McMahon 5, Molby 1, Nicol 6, Rosenthal 7, Rush 18, Whelan 1, Own goals 1.

Steve McMahon lets fly at the QPR goal during a 1990 encounter at Anfield. Liverpool won the game 2-1 and went on to win the League Championship to give Kenny Dalglish his final trophy as manager.

Opposite above: Peter Beardsley wards off a challenge from Aston Villa's Paul McGrath during the 1989/90 season.

Opposite below: The brilliant John Barnes skips past a Chelsea defender during Liverpool's title-winning 1989/90 season.

The Liverpool title-winning squad, 1990. From left to right, back row: Roy Evans (coach), Peter
Beardsley, Ronny Rosenthal, Gary Gillespie, Jan Molby, Ronnie Whelan, Ian Rush, Gary Albett, John
Barnes, Bruce Grobbelaar. Front row: Steve McMahon, David Burrows, Barry Venison, Alan Hansen,
Steve Nicol,, Ray Houghton, Steve Staunton.

Ronnie Moran, Kenny Dalglish and Roy Evans with the First Division Championship and 'Manager of the Year' trophies, 1990.

Above: Ronny Rosenthal, Ian Rush, Ronnie Whelan, Alan Hansen and John Barnes with the League Championship trophy, 1990.

Opposite: Bobby Robson prepares to present Liverpool manager Kenny Dalglish with the Championship trophy, 1990.

With former Anfield great Graeme Souness now at the helm, Liverpool's 1992 FA Cup win was Souness's only trophy win in his acrimonious three-year stint as manager. Despite the fact that he was recovering from major heart surgery, Souness ignored medical advice and accompanied them to Wembley to face Sunderland. At this stage in their history, Liverpool were no longer the dominant force that had swept all before them for the past thirty years, but they were still expected to outclass Second Division Sunderland. Sunderland had already tasted success against West Ham, Chelsea and Norwich on the way to the final and were confident that the Anfield club would be another First Division scalp. The game, however, went to form and Liverpool ran out comfortable 2-0 winners. Goals from Rush and Thomas gave Liverpool their fifth FA Cup win. It was highly appropriate that on the day that he was given the accolade of leading the team out at Wembley, Liverpool assistant manager Ronnie Moran should guide Liverpool to success in a major competition.

Round 3	Crewe Alexandra (a)	Won 4-0
Round 4	Bristol Rovers (a)	Drew 1-1
Round 4 (replay)	Bristol Rovers (h)	Won 2-1
Round 5	Ipswich Town (a)	Drew 0-0
Round 5 (replay)	Ipswich Town (h)	Won 3-2 (aet)
Semi-final	Portsmouth (Highbury)	Drew 1-1 (aet)
Semi-final (replay)	Portsmouth (Villa Park)	Won 3-1 on penalties after 0-0 draw
Final	Sunderland (Wembley)	Won 2-0

Opposite: Bruce Grobbelaar and Glen Hysen with the League Championship trophy, 1990.

Roy Evans in the famous bootroom at Anfield. Evans took over from Graeme Souness as manager in 1994.

Opposite: Graeme Souness, a magnificent player for Liverpool, but his managerial reign at the club was not as successful. He did, however, lead his team to FA Cup success in 1992.

1994/95
LEAGUE (COCA-COLA) CUP WINNERS

Roy Evans' only success as manager was the 1995 League Cup. Evans was a popular appointment and had been at Anfield since the days of Shankly. But the 2-1 victory over Bolton Wanderers at Wembley was the highlight of Evans' tenure in the Liverpool hot seat. Bolton were a team pushing for promotion to the Premier League, and could boast future star names such as Jason McAteer, Alan Stubbs and Alan Thompson, but it was to be Liverpool's up-and-coming sensation Steve McManaman who shone brightest that day. McManaman was outstanding as he displayed his dazzling dribbling skills to the full. Liverpool's two goals came from the boot of McManaman, the first a superb solo effort as he ran deep from midfield before unleashing a shot past Branagan in the Bolton goal. His second was equally good, as he skipped past a number of challengers before netting Liverpool's second. Bolton fought hard but it was Liverpool and McManaman's day.

Round 2, 1st leg	Burnley (h)	Won 2-0
Round 2, 2nd leg	Burnley (a)	Won 4-1
Round 3	Stoke City (h)	Won 2-1
Round 4	Blackburn Rovers (a)	Won 3-1
Round 5	Arsenal (h)	Won 1-0
Semi-final, 1st leg	Crystal Palace (h)	Won 1-0
Semi-final, 2nd leg	Crystal Palace (a)	Won 1-0
Final	Bolton Wanderers (Wembley)	Won 2-1

Above: Roy Evans on his first morning as manager at Liverpool's Melwood training ground, 1994.

Right: Ronnie Moran, a great servant of Liverpool as both a player and later as a coach for nearly fifty years.

Above: Steve McManaman in action for Liverpool. His goals would win them the League (Coca–Cola) Cup in 1995

Opposite: The last day of the famous Anfield Kop. After Liverpool played Norwich City on 30 April 1994 it was converted into an all–seater enclosure.

The dashing Steve McManaman takes on the Blackburn Rovers defence during the 1994/95 season. McManaman scored two sensational goals to win the League Cup for Liverpool against Bolton Wanderers later in the campaign.

2000/01
LEAGUE (WORTHINGTON) CUP WINNERS

After a lean period in their pursuit of silverware, manager Gerard Houllier put the smiles back on Liverpudlian faces with a unique treble of trophies in the 2000/01 season. The first was the League Cup, with the final taking place at the Millennium Stadium, Cardiff. Liverpool's opponents, Birmingham City, made the Reds fight every step of the way. The First Division outfit failed to be disheartened by an outstanding Robbie Fowler strike in the 29th minute. Spotting the Birmingham 'keeper off his line, Fowler volleyed a superb goal from outside the box to give Liverpool the lead. Birmingham fought back and after the interval it was the Midlands club who looked the likeliest to score. With the final whistle approaching, Liverpool looked to have held out when Henchoz brought down O'Connor in the penalty area in the third minute of injury time. Darren Purse beat Westerveld from the spot kick to set up extra time. The additional period of play failed to separate the teams and the dreaded penalty shoot-out gave the two sets of fans a nervous finale. It was Liverpool who held their nerve best and they took the trophy 5-4 on penalties. Gerard Houllier had won his first major trophy as manager.

Round 3	Chelsea (h)	Won 2-1 (aet)
Round 4	Stoke City a)	Won 8-0
Round 5	Fulham (h)	Won 3-0 (aet)
Semi-final, 1st leg	Crystal Palace (a)	Lost 1-2
Semi-final, 2nd leg	Crystal Palace (h)	Won 5-0
Final	Birmingham City (Millennium Stadium, Cardiff)	Won 5-4 on penalties after 1-1 draw

Right: Gerard Houllier, the manager who would lead Liverpool to an incredible treble of major trophies in the 2000/01 season.

Below: Phil Thompson, a great servant to Liverpool as a player and an admirable assistant to Gerard Houllier during Liverpool's fabulous 2000/01 season.

The good times certainly came back to Anfield with a bang in season 2000/01, and after wins against Rotherham, Leeds, Manchester City, Tranmere and Wycombe, Liverpool faced the might of Arsenal in the FA Cup final. For the first time in the competition's history the two finalists were managed by foreign managers. Arsenal boss Arsenal Wenger, with the outstanding French trio of Henry, Viera and Pires in his team line-up, was confident of success. But it would be English football's current superstar Michael Owen who would be winning all the plaudits at the end of the game. In the first FA Cup final ever to be played outside England, it was the London club who looked the likely winners and it was no surprise to see Ljungberg give Arsenal the lead in the second half. There looked to be no way back for Liverpool but Owen, in a six-minute spell that saw the Reds turn the game on its head, scored two magnificent goals to break the hearts of the Arsenal team and their supporters who already thought they had one hand on the trophy. The clinical finishing power of Michael Owen had given his team their second major silverware of the season.

Round 3	Rotherham United (h)	Won 3-0
Round 4	Leeds United (a)	Won 2-0
Round 5	Manchester City (h)	Won 4-2
Round 6	Tranmere Rovers (a)	Won 4-2
Semi-final	Wycombe Wanderers (Villa Park)	Won 2-1
Final	Arsenal (Millennium Stadium, Cardiff)	Won 2-1

Opposite: Robbie Fowler. Fowler's fantastic goal in the League (Worthington) Cup final against Birmingham City in 2001 was one of the highlights of the season for Liverpool fans.

Michael Owen celebrates with Heskey, Gerrard and Fowler after his goal had won the 2001 FA Cup final against Arsenal. Owen scored two goals in a six-minute spell to turn the game on its head. Liverpool ran out 2-1 winners.

The Liverpool team huddle that became a feature of their pre-match rituals during the 2000/01 season.

Liverpool's final piece of silverware in an unforgettable 2000/01 season of treble success was the UEFA Cup. It was the Reds' first European trophy since being crowned European Cup winners in 1984. Liverpool's path to the final had not been easy, and they took some notable scalps on the way. In particular, European giants AS Roma and Barcelona provided stern opposition for Houllier's men, but both were seen off after tense encounters to set up a final against the relatively unknown CD Alaves from Spain. Alaves may have been European minnows, but they put up a determined display in one of the most memorable European finals of all time. Liverpool's 5-4 victory gave them their seventh major European trophy, a total surpassed only by Real Madrid and Barcelona. The final itself was described by some commentators as an 'epic'. Every time Liverpool looked to be in control, the Spanish side would fight back, and at the end of full time the scoreline stood at 4-4. In the first European final to be decided by the Golden Goal rule, a Geli own goal gave the trophy to Liverpool. Alaves at the time were down to nine men after Magno and Karmona were sent off. Gerard Houllier had equalled Joe Fagan's achievement in winning three major trophies in one season.

Round 1, 1st leg	Rapid Bucharest (a)	Won 1–0
Round 1, 2nd leg	Rapid Bucharest (h)	Drew 0–0
Round 2, 1st leg	Slovan Liberec (h)	Won 1–0
Round 2, 2nd leg	Slovan Liberec (a)	Won 3–2
Round 3, 1st leg	Olympiakos (a)	Drew 2–2
Round 3, 2nd leg	Olympiakos (h)	Won 2–0
Round 4, 1st leg	AS Roma (a)	Won 2–0
Round 4, 2nd leg	AS Roma (h)	Lost 0–1
Round 5, 1st leg	FC Porto	Drew 0–0
Round 5, 2nd leg	FC Porto	Won 2–0
Semi-final, 1st leg	Barcelona (a)	Drew 0–0
Semi-final, 2nd leg	Barcelona (h)	Won 1–0
Final	CD Alaves (Dortmund)	Won 5–4 (aet)

Above: Emile Heskey, seen here in action against AS Roma, scored several vital goals during the early rounds of Liverpool's UEFA Cup campaign during the 2000/01 season.

Opposite: Gerard Houllier is jubilant after Liverpool beat CD Alaves of Spain to win the 2001 UEFA Cup final in Dortmund.

2001/02
EUROPEAN SUPER CUP WINNERS

Liverpool defeated the might of Bayern Munich 3–2 in Monaco to take the European Super Cup for the second time in their history. The game between the holders of the Champions League and the UEFA Cup trophies took place at the Stade Louis XI ground in August 2001. As defending European champions, Bayern were favourites to win the one-off game, but goals from Riise, Heskey and Owen took the cup back to Anfield. For much of the match Bayern looked distinctly disinterested, and it was Liverpool who seized the initiative, with their English international trio of Owen, Gerrard and Heskey showing outstanding form. It was only after Liverpool went into a 3–0 lead that the Germans woke up, and goals from Salihamadzic and Jancker gave the fans a grandstand finish. Extra time looked on the cards, but Liverpool held out for a fine victory. The Reds had repeated their European Super Cup success of 1978.

Goalscorers: Riise, Heskey, Owen.

Liverpool team: Westerveld, Babbel, Henchoz, Hyypia, Carragher, Gerrard (Biscan), McAllister, Hamman, Riise (Murphy), Owen (Fowler) Heskey.

Bayern Munich team: Kahn, Sagnol, Lizarazu, Thiam, R. Kovac, Pizarro (Jancker), Linke, Salihamadzic (Santa Cruz), Hargreaves, Sforza (Nkovac), Elber.

Opposite: Sami Hyypia, a rock in defence for Liverpool during their treble season of 2000/01.

Left: Michael Owen, his goals have been vital in Liverpool's trophy-winning exploits of recent years.

Liverpool fans celebrate their team's fantastic treble of trophies during the club's homecoming tour of the city in 2001. (Photograph courtesy of Ian Kemp)

The triumphant Liverpool team parade through the city, 2001. (Photograph courtesy of Martin Reece)

Opposite: Michael Owen, who was outstanding in Liverpool's 3-2 European Super Cup victory over Bayern Munich in 2001.

2002/03
LEAGUE (WORTHINGTON) CUP WINNERS

Gerard Houllier told his players before the start of the 2003 League Cup final against Manchester United to win it for his team's loyal supporters. Against all the football pundits' predictions, Liverpool did as their boss implored and beat United 2-0 at the Millennium Stadium. It was Liverpool's third major final at the Cardiff venue, and after goals by Gerrard and Owen, their one hundred percent record was still intact. A strangely lethargic United, who only a few days earlier had thrashed Italian giants Juventus in a Champions League encounter, could not get to grips with Liverpool. In midfield, the game was billed as the battle of the hardmen, with Keane for United and Gerrard for Liverpool expected to lock horns in a tussle for supremacy. The anticipated clash of the midfield warriors failed to ignite as Liverpool won quite comfortably in the end against a United team who would go on to win the League Championship in some style, but who failed dismally to display their obvious talents on the day. Gerard Houllier had won his fourth major trophy as Liverpool's manager.

Round 3	Southampton (a)	Won 3-1
Round 4	Ipswich Town (h)	Drew 1-1 Won 5-4 on penalties
Round 5	Aston Villa (a)	Won 4-3
Semi-final, 1st leg	Sheffield United (a)	Lost 1-2
Semi-final, 2nd leg	Sheffield United (h)	Won 2-0 (aet)
Final	Manchester United (Millennium Stadium, Cardiff)	Won 2-0

Opposite: Steven Gerrard, who opened the scoring for Liverpool in their 2-0 victory over Manchester United in the 2003 League (Worthington) Cup final. Michael Owen scored Liverpool's other goal.

Selected Sports Titles
by Tempus Publishing

CRICKET

| Lord's: The Cathedral of Cricket | Stephen Green | 0 7524 2167 0 |

FOOTBALL

Aston Villa	Tony Matthews	0 7524 3123 4
Billy Steel: Scotland's Midfield Maestro	Bob MacAlinden	0 7524 2874 8
Brian Harris Story	Chris Westcott	0 7524 2696 6
Bristol Rovers: Definitive History	Stephen Byrne & Mike Jay	0 7524 2717 2
Cards on the Table:	Clive Youlton	0 7524 2580 3
Woking, The Conference Years		
Cheltenham Town FC	Peter Matthews	0 7524 2730 X
Crewe Alexandra Greats	Harold Finch	0 7524 3088 2
Doncaster Rovers Greats	Peter Tuffrey	0 7524 2707 5
Everton: In the 1980s	Phil Thompson	0 7524 2952 3
	& Steve Hale	
Home Park Voices	John Lloyd	0 7524 2949 3
Leed United Champions 1991/92	David Saffer	0 7524 3112 9
Leeds United's Rolls Royce: Paul Madely Story	David Saffer	0 7524 3071 8
Portsmouth FC 2002/03:	Richard Owen	0 7524 2935 3
Pompey's Rise to the Premiership		
Sheffield Wednesday	Nick Johnson	0 7524 2720 2
Tottenham Hotspur since 1953		0 7524 2924 8
Waiting for the Whistle	Andrew Waldon	0 7524 3055 6
West Brom 1953/54 (Season to Remember)	Tony Matthews	0 7524 3124 2
West Ham: Founded on Iron	Brian Belton	0 7524 2928 0
Willie Maley: Man who Made Celtic	David W. Potter	0 7524 2691 5
Wolves against the World	John Shipley	0 7524 2944 7
Workington FC	Nick Eade	0 7524 2818 7

RACING

| Festival Gold: Cheltenham Gold Cup | Stewart Peters | 0 7524 2817 9 |

RUGBY LEAGUE

| Rugby League Hall of Fame | Robert Gate | 0 7524 2693 1 |

SPEEDWAY

Speedway: Prewar Years	Robert Bamford	0 7524 2749 0
Speedway: Through the Lens of Mike Patrick	Mike Patrick	0 7524 2596 X
Wizard of Balance: Peter Craven Story	Brian Burford	0 7524 2856 X